# HENRY FORD

*Essential Lives*

# HENRY

## FORD

### MANUFACTURING MOGUL

by M. J. York

Content Consultant:
John Heitmann
Professor of History, University of Dayton

# ABDO
Publishing Company

# CREDITS

Published by ABDO Publishing Company, 8000 West 78th Street, Edina, Minnesota 55439. Copyright © 2011 by Abdo Consulting Group, Inc. International copyrights reserved in all countries. No part of this book may be reproduced in any form without written permission from the publisher. The Essential Library™ is a trademark and logo of ABDO Publishing Company.

Printed in the United States of America,
North Mankato, Minnesota
052010
092010

♻ THIS BOOK CONTAINS AT LEAST 10% RECYCLED MATERIALS.

Editor: Amy Van Zee
Copy Editor: Susan Freese
Interior Design and Production: Emily Love
Cover Design: Emily Love

**Library of Congress Cataloging-in-Publication Data**
York, M. J., 1983–
  Henry Ford : manufacturing mogul / by M.J. York.
     p. cm.
  Includes bibliographical references and index.
  ISBN 978-1-61613-514-0
  1. Ford, Henry, 1863–1947—Juvenile literature. 2. Automobile industry and trade—United States—Biography—Juvenile literature. 3. Industrialists—United States—Biography—Juvenile literature. 4. Mass production—United States—Juvenile literature. 5. Assembly-line methods—Juvenile literature. I. Title.
  TL140.F6Y67 2011
  338.7'629222092—dc22
  [B]
                                        2010000566

# TABLE OF CONTENTS

| | | |
|---|---|---|
| Chapter 1 | The Race | 6 |
| Chapter 2 | A Born Mechanic | 14 |
| Chapter 3 | Early Successes and Failures | 24 |
| Chapter 4 | The Model T | 34 |
| Chapter 5 | The Assembly Line | 44 |
| Chapter 6 | The Five-Dollar Day | 54 |
| Chapter 7 | Ups and Downs | 64 |
| Chapter 8 | Hard Times | 74 |
| Chapter 9 | The Slow Descent | 86 |
| Timeline | | 96 |
| Essential Facts | | 100 |
| Additional Resources | | 102 |
| Glossary | | 104 |
| Source Notes | | 106 |
| Index | | 109 |
| About the Author | | 112 |

*Henry Ford and driver Barney Oldfield with
the four-cylinder 999 race car circa 1904*

# THE RACE

It was October 10, 1901, and 38-year-old Henry Ford needed to win the race. The previous winter, Ford's Detroit Automobile Company had folded. Ford had disappointed his stockholders by failing to produce a car that could be sold to the public. An unstoppable tinkerer, Ford had trouble knowing when he needed to quit fine-tuning the design and go into production. The delivery truck Ford's company did sell was poorly made and cost more to make than its sticker price. On top of everything, instead of concentrating on creating a sellable model, Ford had been spending the stockholders' money on making a race car!

When the company folded, most of the investors left. Actually, Ford was glad to see them go. He distrusted businesspeople and bankers, and he frowned on anyone who claimed a stake in the company just to make money. Ford did not want investors to interfere with his ideas for producing a car. He wanted his car to be perfect, and he wanted his car to be fast.

A master of publicity, Ford knew that winning automobile races would make people excited about his designs. Enough investors kept their faith in Ford that he was able to complete his racing model in 1901. He had to win the big race in October, or his career in cars would likely be finished.

October 10 was a perfect day for a race. Eight thousand people crammed into the racecourse at Grosse Pointe, Michigan, a short distance from

## Gas versus Steam versus Electric

At the dawn of the automotive age, cars had three types of engines: steam, electric, or gas. In the early days, racers and mechanics chose steam engines, which were heavy but powerful. Wealthy women often chose electric cars because the engines were quiet and clean.

However, the noisy, dirty, gasoline-powered car won out. Electric cars could go only a short range between charges. Cars powered by steam needed large quantities of water and could overheat and explode. Gasoline engines were safer than steam and far less expensive. They also had the potential for greater range and speed than the electrical technology of the time allowed. Before long, steam and electric cars had disappeared from the roads, and gasoline had become the fuel of choice.

Detroit. Businesses locked their doors, and even the courthouse was closed for the event. In this festive atmosphere, families watched a parade of 100 cars of various types: gasoline, steam, and electric powered. Each type of car in several different size classes would compete in the multiple races of the day— electric- and steam-powered cars were much slower than those powered by gasoline. Ford's 2,200-pound (1,000-kg) gasoline-powered car would appear in the final race, the championship event.

Ford's loud, roaring car, the 999, had four large cylinders. A powerful car for the time, it had completed one-half mile (0.8 km) in 26 seconds, which was close to the world record for speed. Ford and his assistant mechanics had made improvements to the design of the axles and the engine. The car was basically an engine on wheels, with

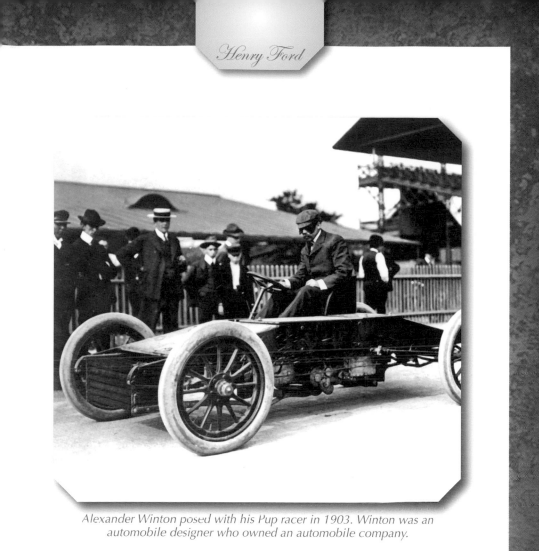

*Alexander Winton posed with his Pup racer in 1903. Winton was an automobile designer who owned an automobile company.*

an unprotected bench for the driver to perch on. For the October 10 race, Ford would drive the car himself.

Ford was the underdog in the 10-mile (16-km) championship race. Two of the original entries had dropped out. That left Ford alone to challenge Alexander Winton, the most famous automobile

### Alexander Winton

By 1901, Alexander Winton was already a famous car racer and producer. Based in Cleveland, Ohio, Winton was one of the earliest car manufacturers in the United States. In 1897, he had driven one of his cars from Cleveland to New York City to show its durability. In 1903, a Winton automobile made the first transcontinental automobile trip from San Francisco, California, to New York City.

Winton held many patents in automobile design. One of his ideas was to move the engine from under the car to the front of the car. He also developed the steering wheel to replace the handle that steered the earliest cars. Ford beat Winton using Winton's own steering wheel design. Although Winton's automobile company could not compete in the industry by the 1920s, his engine company was successful. General Motors bought it in 1930.

racer in the United States. Winton was sure he would win. Supposedly, he had already picked out a spot in his house to display the prize, an expensive glass punch bowl. As for Ford, he had never driven his car on a racetrack before.

The cars rolled up to the starting line. One of Ford's mechanics, "Spider" Huff, hung off the passenger side of the car. He would act as a counterweight to keep the car from tipping over as it sped around the track's tight turns.

In a flash, the cars were off. Winton took an early lead, using his experience to gain ground with every turn. Ford, a quick learner, figured out the turns by the third mile and was soon gaining on Winton. By the seventh mile, the cars were neck and neck. Winton's engine began to smoke. With his mechanically troubled car, he stood no chance against Ford, who shot ahead and won by three-quarters of a mile. Ford had averaged 45 miles per hour (72 km/h), an incredibly fast pace for the time.

Clara Ford, Henry's wife, described the crowd's reaction in a letter to her brother. "The people went wild," she wrote. "One man threw his hat up and when it came down he stamped on it, he was so excited."[1]

The publicity generated by the event was huge. Ford would keep making headlines throughout his career. He understood that making a name

### The First Automobiles

Henry Ford did not invent the automobile. The idea of a so-called horseless carriage had captured people's imaginations since the invention of the steam engine in 1712. The first locomotives went into use in the early eighteenth century, but inventors continued to work on a vehicle that did not need to run on rails. A steam-powered vehicle was developed in France in 1769. By the second half of the nineteenth century, scientists working individually in Europe and the United States were making more steam-powered cars, but they were not producing these cars in mass quantities.

According to most sources, the first truly gasoline-powered car was made by Carl Benz in 1885 in Germany. In the United States, the first successful gasoline-powered car, which was essentially a carriage with an engine attached, was built by Charles and Frank Duryea in 1893. Ford finished his first car three years later. By the time of the race in 1901, hundreds of car companies had sprung up around the country.

Whether gas-, electric-, or steam-powered, automobiles were soon objects of desire for the wealthy. However, it was not until Ford made an affordable car that people of the middle and lower classes were able to enjoy the freedom of the open road.

"I will build a motor car for the great multitude. It will be large enough for the family but small enough for the individual to run and care for. It will be constructed of the best material, by the best men to be hired, after the simplest designs that modern engineering can devise. But it will be so low in price that no man making a good salary will be unable to own one."[2]

*—Henry Ford*

for himself in the race would allow him to continue doing what he saw as his true life's work: getting the entire nation on wheels. It would take determination and perseverance, but Henry Ford was up to the challenge.

*Henry Ford was an innovator in the automobile industry.*

*Henry Ford's birthplace in Michigan circa 1922*

# A BORN MECHANIC

Henry Ford was born on July 30, 1863, during the American Civil War. His parents, William and Mary Ford, lived on a farm near Dearborn, Michigan. Henry grew up doing farm chores and exploring the fields and the forests.

Later in life, Henry wrote about his earliest memory, when he was almost three years old:

> *The first thing I remember in my life is my father taking my brother John and myself to see a bird's nest under a large oak log. . . . I remember the nest with 4 eggs and also the bird and hearing it sing. I have always remembered the song.*[1]

Henry grew up loving nature and rural life. He also grew up knowing how difficult farm life could be. He hated inefficiency. He became interested in machinery because he wanted to make work easier for people.

## Early Interests

Henry started his formal education in a one-room schoolhouse when he was seven. Previously, his mother had taught him the basics of reading. At the schoolhouse, he learned writing and arithmetic. More than anything, however, Henry liked to take things apart so he could see how they worked. His younger siblings—John, Margaret, Jane, William Jr., and

### McGuffey's Readers

Much of Henry's education came from a set of popular nineteenth-century schoolbooks known as McGuffey's *Eclectic Readers*. These books taught morals, including honesty and a strong work ethic, while developing reading and other basic skills. As an adult, Henry believed that much of his character had been formed by reading these books. In the 1920s, he began collecting the old readers. Soon, he owned what may have been the largest private collection of McGuffey's *Eclectic Readers* in the United States.

Robert—all kept their toys away from Henry, afraid that he would return them in pieces. His mother encouraged his experiments, however, and gave him a workbench in the kitchen. Watches were one of Henry's early interests. His fascination began when a farmhand took the back off his watch to allow Henry to see its inner workings. Soon, Henry was fixing watches for his neighbors.

## Ford's Parents

William Ford's family emigrated from Ireland to the United States in 1847 during a famine. Upon settling in Michigan, William, his parents, and his extended family of uncles, aunts, and cousins worked hard to establish themselves. William labored as a carpenter and saved his money. He bought land whenever he could and planned on becoming a farmer.

William met his future wife, Mary Litogot, in 1850. Mary was 10 and William was 22 at the time. Orphaned at a young age, Mary was raised by a childless couple who had come to the United States from a village in Ireland only miles from the Fords' old home. In time, the efficient, intelligent, and patient Mary fell deeply in love with the hardworking William. The two married in 1861, when Mary was 22 and William was 34. With land from both their families, the two settled down on a good-sized farm. Their first child died at birth in 1862. Henry was born in 1863.

Henry's childhood was charmed and happy until the spring of 1876. When he was not quite 13 years old, his mother, Mary, was expecting another baby. Something went wrong with the labor, and Mary and the child both died. Mary had been the center of the Ford family. With her death, something changed between Henry and his father, William.

With his mother gone, Henry began to realize that he did not belong on the farm and was not interested in becoming a farmer. Then, a few months after his mother's death, Henry saw something that would change the course of his life. One July day, while riding in a horse-drawn buggy with his father, Henry first saw a vehicle that moved by its own power. Although it was nothing more than a steam engine on wheels, it inspired Henry. As he explained years later in his autobiography, it was that vision that made him want to create machines for transportation.

In 1879, when Henry was 16 years old, he left the farm and moved to Detroit to start his career as a machinist. He wrote in his autobiography that he and his father had fought and that he left the farm without his father's permission. However, other accounts and documents show that William helped Henry get a job and find a home with relatives in the city.

Henry was fired from his first job at a streetcar manufacturer after only six days. His father then helped him find an apprenticeship at the Flower

Brothers' Machine Shop. There, Henry got a basic education in making machines and engines. At night, he repaired watches to earn extra money. After several months, Henry found a job with the Detroit Dry Dock Company, where he learned more about different types of engines.

## Meeting Clara

In 1882, Henry went back to the family farm. After helping to repair a small steam engine on a neighbor's farm, he discovered he had a talent for taking care of this type of engine. Henry left his Detroit job and spent the next several years fixing engines and demonstrating equipment for a farm machine company. At home on the farm, Henry had time to experiment with his own ideas about wheeled machines. A few years later, he also encountered his first gasoline-powered Otto engine, the ancestor of the modern car engine.

At a country dance on January 1, 1885, 21-year-old Henry first met 18-year-old Clara Bryant, the daughter of a local farmer. Henry later told his sister Margaret that he knew right away that Clara was the woman he would marry. The two did not see each other again for some time, but when they met

again, they started going to dances
and parties together. Henry and
Clara were both serious and practical
people, but they both loved music
and dancing. They got along well.

The couple were engaged by the
spring of 1886. They married on
April 11, 1888, after Henry had saved
enough money to give them a good
financial start. William Ford helped
his son by giving the newlyweds a
plot of land, where they built a nice
house. The couple settled into a
happy first few years of marriage.

## Back to Detroit

Although the newlyweds were
comfortable in their country home,
Ford could not stop dreaming about
machines. He began to envision
a horseless carriage—some type of
transportation that needed neither horses nor tracks
to move. Henry and Clara discussed their future.
Finally, in 1891, the couple decided to give up their
first home and move to Detroit.

"Dear Clara

I again take the pleasure of writing you a few
lines. It seems like a year
since I saw you. . . . Clara
Dear you did not expect
me Friday night and I
think as the weather is so
bad, you will not expect
me tonight. . . . Clara
Dear you can not imagine
what pleasure it gives me
to think that I have at last
found one so loving, kind,
and true as you are and I
hope we will always have
good success. . . .
May Flowerettes of
love around you be
twined
And the Sunshine of
peace shed its joys o'er
your mind
From one that dearly
loves you,
H."[2]

—*Henry Ford to
Clara Bryant during
their courtship
(spelling and punctuation
standardized)*

*Henry Ford in 1888*

Ford quickly found a job with the Edison
Illuminating Company, a business that provided
light and power to the city. Ford saw his position as
a good opportunity to learn more about electricity,
something that he would need to know to make a
better engine. In his free time at work and at home,

Ford worked on his automobile.
On November 6, 1893, Henry
and Clara's only child was born.
They named their son Edsel after a
childhood friend of Henry's.

Less than two months later, on
Christmas Eve, Ford was ready to
test his first homemade gasoline
engine. Although Clara was cooking
a holiday dinner for the family when
Ford dragged the odd machine into
the kitchen, she willingly helped
him start it. It was a two-person
job: Clara had to slowly pour fuel
into the engine as Henry spun the
flywheel. The engine sputtered to
life. Encouraged by this success, Ford
continued his experiments.

## The Quadricycle

Working in his shop with other
mechanics, Ford's model began to
take shape starting in January 1896.
He read a series of articles in the
magazine the *American Machinist* that

**A Primitive Car**

Henry's first car was
basically two bicycles
connected and powered
by a motor. It had no
brakes and could not go
backward. The driver sat
on something similar to
a bicycle seat and steered
with a rod, not a steer-
ing wheel. Instead of a
car horn, the machine
had a doorbell. With the
wooden frame Henry
used to hide the engine,
the Quadricycle looked
very much like a baby
carriage.

gave him new ideas for his engine. The inspiration set off a frantic several months.

Finally, after a 48-hour push with no rest, Ford was ready to test-drive his Quadricycle. Shortly before dawn on June 4, 1896, Clara and Ford's chief assistant, Stephen Bishop, joined Ford to watch the vehicle's triumphant entry onto the streets of Detroit. But when Ford tried to move the Quadricycle out of his shop, he realized that it was too big to fit through the door. The two men worked quickly to take down part of the wall. A short time later, an impatient Ford brought his car out of the shop.

Ford's Quadricycle was a success. It could reach speeds of 20 miles per hour (32 km/h). This success encouraged the young machinist to continue experimenting.

**The First Car in Detroit**

Despite Henry's frantic effort to finish his Quadricycle during the spring of 1896, his car was not the first one driven on the streets of Detroit. That honor went to Charles King, who showed his machine to an admiring crowd on March 6 of that year. King had received formal training as a mechanical engineer at Cornell University and brought those ideas back to Michigan with him. He was even willing to share his secrets with other Detroit mechanics, including Henry. As a triumphant King drove his car at a top speed of five miles per hour (8 km/h) on its first ride, Henry followed behind on his bicycle.

Henry Ford and the Quadricycle in Detroit in 1896

*Henry Ford, top row, third from right, and other employees
of the Edison Illuminating Company*

# EARLY SUCCESSES
## AND FAILURES

Despite Ford's relative success with his first
car, he knew there was much room for
improvement. The Quadricycle could not become
the car of the people. It was too primitive to compete
with the automobiles already available for sale, and

it was too expensive to produce. Even so, Ford did not give up. His belief in the importance of his work and his faith that he was on the right track were both renewed by an event during the summer of 1896.

That year, Ford had a promising career with the Detroit branch of the Edison Illuminating Company. Many of the people he knew thought he was wasting his time toying with automobiles and distracting himself from his career. However, that summer, the Detroit manager invited Ford to a company-wide conference in New York City. At the conference, Ford had the opportunity to meet his biggest hero: Thomas Alva Edison.

The two men discussed Ford's gas-powered engine. Ford sketched his design for the inventor. The ideas excited Edison. As Ford recalled it, Edison banged his hand on the table and offered these words of encouragement:

> *Young man, that's the thing! . . . You have it. Keep at it.*
> *Electric cars must keep near to power stations. . . . Steam*
> *cars won't do either, for they have a boiler and a fire. Your*
> *car is self-contained, carries its own power plant, no fire,*
> *no boiler, no smoke, and no steam. You have the thing.*
> *Keep at it!*[1]

Speaking with Edison was the inspiration Ford needed. As he later explained, "That bang on the table was worth worlds to me. . . . Out of the clear sky the greatest inventive genius in the world had given me a complete approval."[2]

### CONTINUED EFFORTS

Following hard work from the men in his shop, Ford's second car was ready for testing early in 1898. The improved vehicle was much more stylish and elegant than the first. It attracted Ford's first investor,

### Thomas Alva Edison

Thomas Alva Edison was a prolific inventor. He held more than 1,000 patents.

Edison was born on February 11, 1847, in Milan, Ohio. His family moved to Port Huron, Michigan, when he was seven years old. Edison was a smart child but often sick, and he did not do well in school. His mother took him out of school after only a few months and taught him herself.

While a teenager, Edison improved existing inventions and created inventions of his own. He made improvements to the telegraph and the telephone, and he invented the phonograph—the first device for recording sound—in 1877. The light bulb had already been invented, but it did not work well enough to be used in the home. By 1879, Edison had changed that, improving the light bulb and creating a system so homes could be electrified and lighted. Edison formed various electric companies around the country, including the Edison Illuminating Company in Detroit, where Ford worked. Another major Edison invention was a system to record and play back motion pictures.

Later in life, Ford and Edison became good friends and went camping together. Edison's health began to fail in the 1920s, and he died on October 18, 1931.

Detroit Mayor William Maybury, who helped Ford get a loan to buy materials. Ford's third car, released in 1899, attracted the attention of William Murphy, a wealthy businessman who would prove to be one of Ford's most important early investors.

A number of other investors followed Murphy, and it seemed that Ford's Detroit Automobile Company was off to a great start. Although Ford was offered a promotion and a raise at the Edison Illuminating Company, he quit his job ten days after forming his new company. Sadly, as the months wore on and Ford could not produce a car for public sale, most of his investors pulled out. The company ultimately closed during the winter of 1900–1901.

Murphy still had faith in Ford, however. He continued to support the carmaker's efforts through the car race in October 1901. He also supported the formation of a second company, the Henry Ford Company, founded in November 1901. Unfortunately for Murphy, Ford was still focusing his attention on race cars. In the spring of 1902, Murphy hired another mechanic to see what Ford was doing. Upset by the interference, Ford left the company. With this move, he lost his connection to his biggest investor.

**First Driver's License**

At the time Ford drove his first experimental cars around the streets of Detroit, the concept of having a driver's license did not exist. A system for making sure drivers actually knew how to drive was unnecessary, as there were so few cars. In 1897, Detroit Mayor Maybury issued to Ford what historians consider to be the first driver's license. Ford did not have to take a test to make sure he could drive well. Instead, the license gave him permission to make noise on public streets with his loud vehicle.

The collapse of the second company confirmed Ford's distrust of businesspeople. He felt that Murphy's actions proved that investors were more concerned with short-term profit than long-term success. Ford believed his investors were not willing to give him enough time to experiment and make the best product. Instead, they wanted to push a car into production and make the quickest, largest profit possible. Ford needed to find someone who would back him financially while he worked out his designs.

The race cars became Ford's lifeline. He found new investors to back his ventures—investors who were obsessed with racing. He also found a driver, Barney Oldfield, to take over on the racetrack in Ford's powerful new car, the 999. Oldfield was a fearless bicycle racer who was happy to switch to cars. In the next few years, Oldfield drove Ford's cars to victory in many races. Ford knew he could turn the

*A Ford Motor Company factory in Detroit, Michigan, circa 1903*

positive publicity into sales. Now, he just needed a commercial car to sell to the public.

## Ford's ABCs

On August 16, 1902, the Ford Motor Company was born. Alexander Malcomson was the first investor, and he formed a partnership with Ford. The businessman was a huge racing fan. He had become enthusiastic about Ford's designs after the carmaker's victory over Winton the previous year.

## James Couzens

James Couzens was born in 1872 in Ontario, Canada, just across the border from Detroit. Trained as a bookkeeper, he worked for several companies before going to work for Alexander Malcomson and becoming part of the Ford Motor Company.

Couzens's bookkeeping skills were essential to the success of the young company, because Ford had no patience for paperwork. Couzens paid bills, tracked sales, and hired and fired workers. For many years, he was one of the most important people in the company. In 1915, Ford's politics and personality drove Couzens out of the company. The bookkeeper later had a successful political career, first as the mayor of Detroit and later as a senator from Michigan. He died in 1936.

Malcomson had a plan for keeping Ford on track with production. Unlike Ford's previous two companies, the Ford Motor Company would share its profits among the owners. Ford would only get paid if the company were profitable. Malcomson sent his clerk, James Couzens, to be the new company's bookkeeper. The efficient young man soon became a key player in the company.

By the spring of 1903, the Ford Motor Company had set up a large shop for its ten workers to assemble vehicles. Ford had also completed the design for his first commercial vehicle: the Model A. This success attracted enough investors that Ford and Malcomson were able to legally incorporate the company on June 16, 1903. Incorporation is a legal name for a business owned by a group of people. That summer, the company's workers made the first Model A automobiles for sale to the public. With sales of the first cars in July, the company was up and running. In 1904, the company had outgrown its first production plant. By 1905, the company had almost 300 employees and had moved to a new factory. The workers could build approximately 25 cars in a day.

Between 1903 and 1906, the Ford Motor Company rolled out a number of models. The cars reflected the differing viewpoints of Ford and Malcomson. The Model A, Model C, Model F, and Model N fit Ford's vision of light, inexpensive, no-frills cars for the general public. In Ford's view, the company would sell more cars, but make less profit on each sale. In contrast, the Model B and Model K were more luxurious, powerful, and expensive. They appealed to Malcomson's desire to sell at high profit margins. Malcomson was willing to sell fewer models. However, each sale would bring in a large profit.

**An Icy Record**

In January 1904, the Model B was selling slowly. Ford knew that winning a race would increase interest in the car, so he put a Model B engine in a race car and set out to break the world speed record. He chose a dramatic location for the event: the surface of a frozen lake. Burning cinders were spread over the ice to create traction and help keep the car from slipping.

Ford drove the race car himself this time, although his old helper, "Spider" Huff, held down the accelerator while Ford steered. The pair sped across the icy lake, skidding and bouncing the whole way. Their top speed was more than 100 miles per hour (161 km/h), a new record.

Soon, these different viewpoints created serious clashes between the company's two leaders. They began to disagree on everything. By July 1906, Couzens had helped Ford outsmart Malcomson and take over the company. When Malcomson and several other original investors sold their shares, Ford bought them. As the stockholder with the most shares, Ford gained control of the company's future.

*Clara Bryant Ford and a friend drove a Model N Ford.*

*Henry Ford with his son, Edsel, in a Model F Ford in 1905*

# THE MODEL T

ord was driven by his vision of the future. He believed that an ordinary family should be able to afford an automobile and other newly invented consumer goods. As biographer Steven Watts explains, "[Ford] understood that, whereas thrift and self-control had been the hallmarks of success in an earlier age, spending and self-fulfillment were becoming the cultural lubricant that kept the mass society of the new century moving ahead smoothly."[1] Buying and consuming were becoming increasingly important to more Americans. Ford's company would take advantage of the rising middle class's desire to purchase. Most importantly, Ford would give people the power to go where they wanted, when they wanted.

The Model N, launched in 1906, was Ford's first smash success. At a time when the average car was a luxury vehicle that sold for more than $2,000, the simple Model N started at a cost of just $500. Although the car featured top-of-the-line mechanicals, almost everything except the car horn cost extra. For instance, if the buyer wanted a roof on the car, it cost $30 to $50 more. Selling

"You know, Henry . . . your car lifted us out of the mud. It brought joy into our lives. We loved every rattle in its bones."[2]

—*Letter from a Georgia farm wife to Henry Ford, 1918*

more than 8,500 cars that year, Ford outdid his two nearest competitors combined.

In 1907, Ford introduced the Model R and Model S. With improved features and updated bodies, these new models were slightly better versions of the Model N. Models N, R, and S were all quite popular. Even so, their successes were far exceeded in 1908 by an extraordinary sensation: the Model T.

## THE KEY TO THE T

The Model T was made possible by a new metal alloy, or mixture of two metals. As Ford told the story, he was at a race in 1905 when he went to examine the engine of a French Peugeot car that had crashed. The European model used small amounts of a metal that was lighter but stronger than anything made in the United States. Ford investigated the mystery metal. He knew that it would make his cars lighter and stronger and therefore faster and safer.

Ford set up a steel company to experiment with the alloy, known as vanadium steel. His company was the first in the nation to produce it. Engineer Harold Wills became Ford's expert on the metal. It was gradually added to the design of the Model N.

However, it was not widely used until production of the Model T.

Also crucial to the success of the Model T was Charles Sorensen, whom Ford hired in 1905. Sorensen was one of several gifted engineers hired by the automaker. Ford and his engineering staff made sketches and notes on a chalkboard to determine the designs for each part of the car. Sorensen then put these ideas into blueprints for production. Because Ford did not like to read blueprints, Sorensen also made three-dimensional models. The models let Ford see

### Ford Mechanics and Engineers

Ford's number-one mechanic and right-hand man was Harold Wills. Trained as a mechanic and engineer, Wills drafted plans for Ford as early as 1899. Of all the men on staff at Ford Motor Company, Wills was somewhat of a personal friend of Ford. In the early days, Wills and Ford spent many late nights in the shop together. Wills was strong enough to stand up to Ford's forceful personality. He stuck to his own design ideas when he thought he was right. Wills worked with vanadium steel and helped design the Model T's new transmission.

Wills left the company in 1919 when another engineer, Charles Sorensen, won a power struggle between the two men. Sorensen was also involved in the design of the Model T. However, he believed his role in the company was to interpret what Ford wanted and then make it happen, no matter what. Sorensen thought anyone who contradicted Ford, such as Wills, had to be stopped. People within Ford Motor Company were afraid of Sorensen because of his bad temper. His ongoing conflicts with other managers added to the company's struggles during the 1920s.

*Three women in a Model T, circa 1908*

and feel exactly how each part would work. Ford's cars could not have been created without the talented people who worked for him.

### THE FINISHED PRODUCT

When the Model T was rolled out in October 1908, it offered more value for the dollar than any other car on the market. It was not the cheapest car, but its fine engineering made it well worth the investment. Huge improvements had been made in the transmission and engine of the Model T. Its mechanical workings were all covered by vanadium steel. Each part of the car was produced exactly the same way and therefore performed similarly. Uniform production was essential in mass production. Ford was a man of efficiency, and he thought hard about a system that would allow him to produce many cars in a consistent manner. At an initial price of $850, the car lived up to its advertisements, which proclaimed, "No car under $2,000 offers more."[3]

Like earlier Fords, the Model T was sold without frills: the speedometer, windshield, and doors had to be purchased separately. The original car came only in green; later, the primary color was switched to black. Ford famously stated, "Any customer can have a car painted any color that he wants so long as it is black."[4] The Model T's light, flexible steel made it tough enough to withstand the rutted, muddy

### Customize Your Model T

The Model T was sold totally stripped down—"naked as a baby," as author E. B. White described it.[5] Yet mechanics and mail-order catalogs quickly began selling add-ons and improvements of all types for the car.

Some owners added necessary equipment, such as lights and reflectors, a rearview mirror, a guard to keep the fan belt on, tire patches, containers for extra oil and gas, rubber antirattling attachments, and shock absorbers. Other drivers added all kinds of decorative touches: door handles, flower vases, hood ornaments, and even "a . . . vase guaranteed, according to Sears, to fill the car with a 'faint clean odor of lavender.'"[6]

roads of the turn of the twentieth century. And the simple design of the car meant that most drivers could be their own mechanics. In fact, drivers had to be able to fix most of the Model T's common problems. Otherwise, they risked getting stranded on the nation's primitive roads and long stretches of empty fields and forests.

Of all consumers, farmers were the ideal owners of the Model T. Because it was strong enough for country driving, the Model T made what had been a half-day or all-day trip to town by horse and wagon into a quick ride of an hour or two. Having a Model T helped farm families feel less isolated. At times, the automobile even helped with work on the farm. Ford loved to show how to pop a wheel off the Model T, attach a belt to its axle, and power farm machines with it in place of a generator.

## Nicknames and Jokes

By the 1910s, the Model T was a huge part of the U.S. culture and consciousness. The car was known as Tin Lizzie, Flivver, Jalopy, and Hunka Tin, and owners often gave their cars personal names. There were also all kinds of Model T jokes:

• "'I hear you have an auto, Frank. What make is it?' 'A Ford.' 'Whatever made you buy a Ford?' 'That's the only one I could a-Ford.'"[7]

• "Why is the Ford like a millionaire baby? Because it has a new rattle every day."[8]

• "A gallon of gasoline and a quart of oil/A piece of wire to make a coil/An old tin can and a piece of board/And there you are, you have a Ford."[9]

## Deep Emotions

The Model T was different from any earlier car because its drivers often became emotionally attached to it. As the first automobile that many people owned, the Model T created fond memories for its millions of drivers. People cried when they sold their Model Ts. Many named their Model Ts and imagined that their cars had human emotions.

This affection might have had something to do with the Model T's special transmission, which made the car strain forward even when it was stopped and then spring to life when the driver touched the accelerator. In 1936, author E. B. White wrote poetically about his love for his old Model T, which he named Hotspur:

> *Even when the car was in a state known as neutral, it trembled with a deep imperative and tended to inch forward. . . . In this respect it was like*

### The Transcontinental Race

In 1909, Ford found a great opportunity to promote his new car. He entered two Model Ts in a race from New York City to Seattle, Washington. The journey east of the Mississippi River was easy. But west of the river and into the mountains, the trip became difficult. The cars plodded over muddy tracks that hardly deserved to be called roads. The drivers faced bad weather, tried to follow inaccurate maps, and found few places to stop for gas. However, the Ford cars made it through the toughest conditions.

Ford was in Seattle to see the end of the race. Of the six entries, only three completed the race. Two of the finishers, including the winner, were Fords.

*a horse, rolling the bit on its tongue, and country people brought to it the same technique they used with draft animals. . . . I can still feel my old Ford nuzzling me at the curb, as though looking for an apple in my pocket.*[10]

In 1908, selling 1,000 cars was considered a huge success. That year, Ford sold nearly 6,000 Model Ts. By 1916, he was selling 575,000 a year. In the mid-1920s, when this model was most popular, more than two-thirds of the cars in the United States were Model Ts. Between 1908 and 1927, approximately 15 million Model Ts were produced.

*Ford needed many workers to meet the popular demand
for the Model T automobile.*

*Workers assembling the bodies of Model T Fords, circa 1915*

# THE ASSEMBLY LINE

By the spring of 1909, less than a year after the Model T had been released, Ford's plant could not keep up with the demand. Ford had to open a new factory. He had plans for a better, faster way of production.

As early as 1903, Ford had realized something important about mass production. "The way to make automobiles," he suggested, "is to make one automobile like another automobile, to make them all alike, . . . just as one pin is like another pin when it comes from a pin factory."[1]

At the beginning of the twentieth century, cars were made individually—and slowly—by skilled machinists and craftspeople. Other industries, however, had found ways to speed up production. Some items were made with identical parts that could be replaced. If one part broke, it could be replaced instead of the entire product. Some industries also divided up the labor needed to make an item. Instead of one person completing every step in making an entire product, different people specialized in different steps of the process. For example, the meat-packing industry used a

## Saving Steps and Saving Time

Influenced by the work of Frederick Winslow Taylor, who created a system to increase factory efficiency, Ford realized the huge impact that small efficiencies could make. He calculated, "Save ten steps a day for each of twelve thousand employees and you will have saved fifty miles of wasted motion and misspent energy."[2] Every minute counted, according to Ford. "How important it is that the utmost care be used to guard against the loss of a minute of a workman's time, can be realized when it is considered that if each of the 16,000 men employed wasted one minute a day the company would be losing about 266 hours of productive labor."[3]

basic assembly line. Each carcass was pulled through the cutting room on a moving chain past the butchers, who cut away their assigned pieces as it moved past them. Eventually, Ford combined all of these concepts into the most efficient production system the world had ever seen.

## HIGHLAND PARK

Ford had always expected to expand the Ford Motor Company. He purchased the land for a huge plant at Highland Park, a Detroit suburb, years before the Model T went into production. By January 1910, the new factory was complete enough for the company to move in. In the past, a typical industrial complex had been made up of a group of small buildings, each with its own function and task. The Highland Park plant was different. All of the work was put under one massive roof. The various

"The man who places a part does not fasten it. . . . The man who puts in a bolt does not put on the nut; the man who puts on the nut does not tighten it."[4]

*—Ford on his assembly line system*

departments were organized on the four floors of
the plant to operate as efficiently as possible. Soon,
15,000 workers
were churning
out Ford cars at a
record rate, helped
by specialized
machines whenever
possible.

The laborers
who assembled
the smaller parts
of the car were
assigned work
stations and had
the materials they
needed brought to
them. When the
time came to put
the smaller parts
together, the car's
base was set on a
stand. The workers
responsible for the
different steps of

## Ford Dealers

One of the early strengths of the Ford Motor
Company was the tight control it kept over its
dealers. At the time, most other car companies
sold their vehicles directly from the factory or
allowed part-time dealers to sell their vehicles
as a side business to their regular jobs. Nearly
anyone could become a car dealer. At the turn
of the century in Colorado, one dealership was
even owned and managed by an 11-year-old
boy.

Ford and James Couzens, however, had
much stricter policies toward dealers. While
most manufacturers allowed dealers to pay
after the cars had been sold, Ford demanded
50 percent of the payment in advance. Hold-
ing less debt allowed the company to charge
a little less for its cars. Ford also wanted to be
able to stand behind the performance of his
vehicles, so he required dealers to be professional and work full-time. This way, dealers
would be available to service the cars they sold
or provide parts at any time.

In return, the Ford Motor Company gave its
dealers a lot of support. The company sent the
marketing director, Norval Hawkins, to visit
dealers and give them sales materials and tips.
The company even published a magazine for
its dealers, *Ford Times*, which featured articles
about effective selling, automobile updates,
dealership openings, and good reviews from
buyers.

*Ford's Highland Park factory made use of the assembly line system.*

the assembly came up to each car to do their parts
and then moved on to the next car. Once the wheels
went on, the car was rolled from station to station.

The original system at Highland Park allowed
production to grow from approximately 20,000
units in 1910 to 50,000 in 1911 and to 80,000 in
1912. However, Ford's greatest idea was yet to come.

## "Taking the Work to the Men"

It is not clear exactly how Ford and his employees came up with the idea of a moving assembly line. Some stories say that Ford was inspired by watching carcasses move past butchers at a meat-packing plant or by seeing workers in a watch factory taking the pieces they needed from a conveyor belt. The assembly line at Highland Park began in small steps. Charles Sorensen said that the managers experimented in 1908 by dragging a car through the plant from station to station with rope. As Ford explained it, "The first step forward in assembly came when we began taking the work to the men instead of the men to the work."[5]

The first assembly line in the Ford plant took shape in April 1913 in the flywheel-magneto department. Workers stood around a long, smooth-topped table. After each worker completed his task, he slid the growing part to his neighbor. Soon, workers began to use a chain to pull the parts along at a fixed speed. This made the process more efficient by regulating the workflow: slow workers had to speed up and fast workers slowed down. The time it took to produce a flywheel magneto dropped from twenty minutes to five. Quickly, the system spread to other departments that made parts.

To keep up with the faster production of parts, Ford had to apply the system to the assembly of the entire car. As historian Steven Watts explains,

> *In the public mind, it became the Ford assembly line, with its image of a conveyor belt some hundred yards long, relentlessly moving the chassis [car frame] along as nearly two hundred workers performed a series of tasks, each adding parts and components to the whole, until, at the end, the radiator was filled, the engine started, and the completed car driven off to the holding lots.* [6]

The assembly line changed everything. Before, it had taken 12 hours and 28 minutes to put together an entire car. In the summer of 1914, using the assembly line system, a car could be assembled in 1 hour and 33 minutes.

### Showing the Public

In 1915, Ford used the Panama-Pacific International Exposition in San Francisco, California, to show off his new system. He put on display a short version of the assembly line. Parts were brought in so workers could assemble cars from beginning to end, just as they did in the Highland Park factory. At the end of the line, the cars were ready to be driven off. The crowds at the exhibition were so excited that they broke down the safety railing trying to get a better look at the assembly line.

This shortened time made it cheaper to produce each car. In the summer of 1913, even before the system had been put completely in place, Ford lowered the price of a Model T to $500.

## UNHAPPY LABORERS

Making cars using an assembly line greatly increased production. However, as production became more routine during 1913, the workers grew unhappy. Workers who had performed as skilled mechanics were now limited to doing one simple task over and over as quickly as possible. There was no craftsmanship and thus little job satisfaction. Skilled workers who were not promoted quickly left the company. The plant had trouble finding workers and even more trouble keeping them.

This situation created a huge contradiction for Ford. As a young man, he had envisioned that

**Inhuman Speed**

One worker wrote of his bad experiences with the new assembly line system at Ford: "The harried foreman told me that my operation had been timed by an efficiency expert to produce a certain number of finished parts per day. I timed myself to see what I could actually do, and realized that I might achieve the quota only if all went well and I worked without letup the entire eight hours. No allowance was made for lunch, toilet time, or tool sharpening."[7]

machines would improve people's lives and save them from doing dull work. Yet with each improvement in the assembly line, the workers' jobs became less skilled and more boring.

In part because of the company's trouble keeping employees, Ford made his next big move: He created the five-dollar day. ⌐

Ford in his Highland Park office in 1913

*Workers produced flywheel magnetos on the assembly line at Ford's Highland Park factory.*

# THE FIVE-DOLLAR DAY

As business manager James Couzens told the story, it was his revelation during Christmas 1913 that brought about the Ford Motor Company's boldest move yet: the five-dollar day. Ford also took credit for this unprecedented pay increase. Regardless of the source, the announcement of this huge raise in workers' wages meant huge changes in the workplace.

At the time, it was common for companies in the auto industry to lay off workers for several weeks around Christmas. Workers got no pay until production began again the next year. As Couzens watched workers going home to their families with no pay for Christmas, he felt guilty. As he noted, "The company had piled up a huge profit from the labor of these men; the stockholders were rolling in wealth, but all that the workers themselves got was a bare living wage."[1]

Earlier in 1913, some workers had received slightly larger raises than normal. The company had also tried a system of bonus pay that year, but because of how it was set up, most workers did not get any extra money. On January 5, 1914, the Ford Motor Company announced to its workers

**Average Wages**

Five dollars for one day's work was double the standard wage in the auto industry in 1914. This daily wage worked out to 62.5¢ per hour, which was better than the average for many jobs. For instance, in 1914, the average pay for cotton workers was roughly 15¢ per hour; for shoemakers, 21¢ to 24¢ per hour; and for iron and steel workers, 26¢ to 30¢ per hour. Women working in the same industry as men almost always received lower wages. Men working in a unionized factory or business, however, earned higher wages than the average in the industry.

*James Couzens and Henry Ford circa 1910*

that their wages were immediately being raised to $5.00 per day. With the average worker making approximately $2.50 per day, this meant that wages were doubling overnight.

## Why Pay More?

The Ford Motor Company had several reasons for raising wages. First, Ford had trouble keeping workers as the labor on the assembly line became more tedious and boring. As one historian explained, "So great was labor's distaste for the new machine system that toward the close of 1913 every time the company wanted to add 100 men to its factory personnel, it was necessary to hire 963."[2]

Across the United States, a larger battle between labor and management was underway. Labor unions organized for every industry. They led strikes for better working conditions and better pay. Many Americans felt the owners of large corporations were evil and greedy. Often known as robber barons, these businessmen were viewed as growing rich off the labor of their employees without sharing the good fortune.

In contrast, Ford increased wages dramatically and also changed the work day from two nine-hour shifts to three eight-hour shifts. Putting these changes in place not only made Ford seem fair to his workers, but it also increased workers' productivity. Letters from job seekers flooded the mail room at Ford Motor Company. Men came from all over and waited in

### Rioting for Work

Within days of Ford's surprising announcement, more than 10,000 men crowded outside the gates of the Highland Park factory. News had spread that the new three-shift schedule had created 4,000 jobs. But even when these had been snapped up, the crowds kept coming. At first, the men were cheerful and hopeful as they waited in the January cold. But when they realized there were not enough jobs for everyone, they became angry. They broke through the outer wooden fence but were stopped by the sturdy metal fence behind it. Restless and irritated, the crowd blocked Ford's employees from entering the factory.

The police appeared and tried to disperse the crowds with fire hoses. Instead, they were just in time to witness a riot. Men threw bricks and sticks at the plant. Several arrests were made before the situation cooled down.

huge crowds, hoping to find jobs. At the same time, union activity in the company decreased.

The five-dollar day brought about a huge amount of good publicity. Ford's announcement of the wage increase took over newspaper headlines for weeks. It fixed Ford's status as an American hero. People could feel good about buying Ford's cars, because they believed he shared the wealth with his employees. Ford became the shining example of how big business could do good in the world.

As Couzens had noted before the wage increase, the company's huge profits were not helping its workers. With the five-dollar day, Ford and his executives may have really wanted to make their workers happy, in addition to stopping organized labor and garnering good publicity. As Ford announced to newspaper reporters, "We believe in making 20,000 men prosperous and contented rather than follow the plan of making a few slave drivers in our establishment millionaires."[3]

From his earliest days in business, Ford had distrusted investors and felt more connected to farmers and workers. He may also have felt tension between his desire to increase efficiency and his own personal dislike of tedious work. By increasing wages, Ford at least gave his workers more resources to better enjoy their time away from work. Moreover, Ford knew that the new industries and industrialized economy depended on people being able to buy more than life's basic necessities. Giving his workers a pay raise would allow them to become bigger consumers. If other industries followed his example, more people would be able to buy all types of goods.

## Strings Attached

Despite what was announced in the huge "Five-Dollar Day" headlines,

### Other Companies Could Not Keep Up

After Ford announced his dramatic wage increase, the rest of the business community spoke out against it. Many felt that Ford was ruining things for them. No company without Ford's huge profits could afford to pay its workers so much. That meant Ford could draw the best workers away from the other car companies. As the makers of the Packard car complained, "How are we going to avoid paying these wages once you start paying them here in Detroit? We are not running a philanthropic business like you."[4]

In addition, some argued that if all companies wanted to raise wages, they would all have to raise prices to stay in business. Then, nobody would come out ahead. Critics also wondered how workers sharing in their employer's profits would feel if they had to share equally in its losses. At some factories, especially those of the other automakers in Detroit, workers were unhappy because their companies could not or would not meet Ford's new standard.

Ford's success put his company dramatically ahead of his competitors. With the assembly line, in particular, Ford reduced costs so much that he could have afforded raising workers' wages to twenty dollars a day.

"There are thousands of men out there in the shop who are not living as they should. Their homes are crowded and unsanitary. . . . Now, these people are not living in this manner as a matter of choice. Give them a decent income and they will live decently—will be glad to do so. What they need is the opportunity to do better, and someone to take a little personal interest in them—someone who will show that he has faith in them."[5]

—Henry Ford explaining the importance of raising workers' wages

workers needed to meet several possible conditions to receive the full benefit of the raise. The first catch was that the raise was actually a profit-sharing plan. In the first year, the plan was to be an experiment. If the company did not make enough profits, it would cancel the plan the next year. Wages would go back to their original levels. This policy gave workers a huge desire to be more productive. Anyone who did not perform well could be fired and easily replaced. With the success of the Model T and the efficiency of the assembly line, the company's profits skyrocketed. The profit-sharing plan remained in place.

However, there was another catch. When Ford announced the pay increase, he also created what he called a "sociological department" in the company. The stated purpose of the department was to "guard against an employee's prosperity injuring his efficiency."[6] The company wanted to make sure that its workers spent their higher wages in ways that Ford approved of. It soon became clear that to receive the higher wages at all, employees had to have the same values and beliefs as Ford. The sociological department would check up on the employees. It would make sure that they were spending their money and living their lives in ways that met with Ford's approval.

Another condition was that only employees with certain family situations would receive the raise. It was available to "married men living with and taking good care of their families, . . . single men over twenty-two years of age who are of proven thrifty habits, . . . men under 22 years of age, and women who are the sole support of some next of kin."[7] The sociological department would investigate employees and decide who had "thrifty habits" or who was

"At that time, I was boarding, . . . and my folks were living out in the suburbs. The fellow making the investigation did not ask me so many questions; he went around asking other people about me. He even talked to my mother and called the lady that was running the boardinghouse. They really checked on everything before you were paid $5 a day."[8]

*—A Ford employee describing the sociological department's investigation process*

"taking good care of their families." The department made sure that employees did not drink too much or spend their money gambling. It also encouraged employees to open savings accounts and handed out pamphlets on thrifty living. It even gave advice on family life and raising children.

Through the sociological department, Ford was achieving another goal: creating a society where happy families enjoyed the benefits of industrialization. Clean living was a key part of this society. Ford could make his employees live by his standards by paying them high wages and keeping tabs on them. Because of the investigations, Ford had a dependable, sober workforce. At the same time, the investigations kept union activities to a minimum. Ford gave his workers unbelievably high wages, but in return, he took control of their personal lives.

*Applicants gathered outside the Ford Highland Park plant after the announcement of the five-dollar day in 1914.*

*World War I began in Europe in 1914. The United States entered the war in 1917.*

# UPS AND DOWNS

*W*orld War I began in August 1914, after Archduke Franz Ferdinand of Austria was assassinated on June 28. Europe quickly became engulfed in war, as Great Britain, France, and the other Allied powers faced Germany, Austria, and the other Central powers. The United States was sympathetic to the Allies but did not immediately join the fight.

Ford was a pacifist—he wanted the United States to stay out of the war. Unlike some businesspeople, who saw war as an opportunity to make profits, Ford believed that war was a terrible waste of money and manpower. And he was not shy about sharing his opinions.

On May 17, 1915, the Germans sank the British ocean liner *Lusitania*. The ship had been carrying U.S. passengers, and after the attack, many in the United States favored joining the war. Even with popular opinion running against him, Ford continued to state his pacifist views.

Ford's insistence on openly stating his views caused a major rift with one of his most important partners, James Couzens. Couzens was in favor of the United States preparing for war. As Ford used the company's name and publications to broadcast his antiwar platform, Couzens opposed him. Sales suffered as popular opinion turned against Ford.

"I think the people of the world know—even if the politicians do not—that war never settles anything."[1]

—*Henry Ford,*
*My Life and Work*

Whatever Ford's personal views, Couzens did not want him to drag the company into politics. Rather than be associated with Ford's political positions, Couzens left the Ford Motor Company on October 12, 1915.

## PEACE SHIP

In November 1915, Ford met with other peace activists in New York City. Somehow, the group formed the idea that they would hire a ship to travel to Europe, gather together the European leaders for discussion, and end the war immediately. Ford hired the cruise ship *Oscar II* and invited a number of well-known people to join him on the trip. However, few people were interested. No one with a real understanding of the situation believed that the "Peace Ship," as it was called, had any chance of succeeding. Ford had hoped the event would be reported with front-page headlines, but instead, he was mocked in the newspapers.

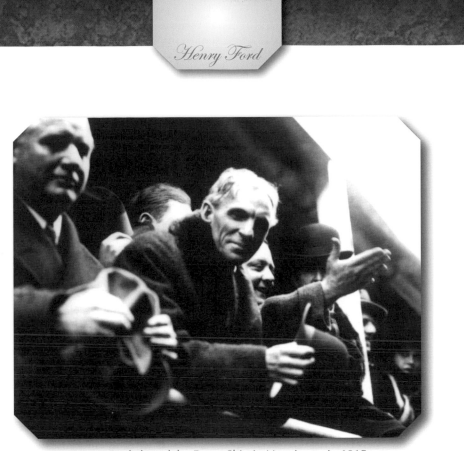

*Henry Ford aboard the Peace Ship in New Jersey in 1915*

The *Oscar II* left port on December 4, 1915. Ford's wife, Clara, thought the whole idea was foolish and refused to go. Most of the passengers went along for the free trip to Europe rather than to support the mission. The most well-known person aboard was Ford himself. As the ship sailed across the Atlantic Ocean, Ford realized the whole plan for peace was unraveling. He left the ship when it docked in Norway and found another ocean liner on which to sail home. The Peace Ship group traveled through Europe but utterly failed at their mission. Despite being ridiculed for his failure, Ford probably benefited from this event in the end. It supported the image of Ford standing up for the people. As the *New York American* explained, "No matter if he failed [to end the war], . . . he at least TRIED."[2]

After the United States declared war on Germany on April 6, 1917, Ford threw his company wholeheartedly into the war effort until the war ended on November 11, 1918. However, the Peace Ship remained an example of how Ford's obsessions sometimes overruled his common sense.

## A Short Career in Politics

In 1918, one of Michigan's seats in the U.S. Senate came open. Ford had contributed a huge sum of money to President Woodrow Wilson's reelection campaign two years earlier. The president returned the favor and asked Ford to consider running for the Senate seat. Ford ran first as a Republican. After losing the Republican primary to Truman Newberry, Ford switched parties and won the Democratic nomination instead. However, while campaigning for the general election, Ford refused to make speeches or spend money. Because of this, most people did not know why he was running or what issues he supported. In addition, Ford's opponent, Newberry, was a former U.S. secretary of war. Newberry's military background was reassuring to voters because the country was still at war. Ford was almost popular enough to overcome these difficulties, but his opponent proved stronger, and Ford lost by a small margin.

At the end of 1918, Ford made a shocking announcement. He would resign from the presidency of Ford Motor Company and turn it over to his son, Edsel. The 25-year-old Edsel had worked for the company since 1912, and he was a capable manager and executive. At first, Edsel was thrilled at the appointment. Before long, however, he learned that his father had no intention of giving up command. Edsel was now the president of Ford Motor Company, but only in name. The elder Ford would continue to make all decisions for years to come.

### Edsel Joins the Company

Edsel Ford got his first car when he was eight and drove himself to school in it. That was the beginning of his love affair with automobiles. Edsel joined the Ford Motor Company in 1912 after high school. He first learned the business by working around the office, and he was quickly promoted. The other executives noticed Edsel's talents as a manager. While the elder Ford was harsh and difficult to work for, Edsel tried to smooth things over and work with people. The father's and son's different personalities would later cause problems between them.

## TAKING CONTROL

In 1919, 40 percent of the cars made in the United States were Fords. Henry Ford wanted to continue to expand the company, but enough stockholders disagreed with him to stall his plans. The stockholders were led by two dissatisfied brothers, John and Horace Dodge. Together, they demanded that the company pay huge dividends. Rather than spend money to expand, the brothers wanted more profit going to the stockholders' pockets. If Ford would not comply, the stockholders wanted Ford to buy out their stock at a high price. Ford refused, knowing that he had control of the majority of the stock.

The stockholders sued Ford in November 1916. He repeatedly refused to buy their stock, not wanting them to get any money as reward for their lawsuit. However, Ford lost the suit in February 1919 and had to pay the dividends.

With this loss, Ford was fed up. Even though he owned a majority of the stock, he now wanted total control of the company. He believed that the profits of a business should serve its customers and its employees, not its shareholders. He explained:

*The stockholders, to my way of thinking, ought to be only those who are active in the business and will regard the company as an instrument of service rather than as a machine for making money. If large profits are made . . . then they should be turned back into the business so that it may be still better fitted to serve, and in part passed on to the purchaser.[3]*

In a clever but dishonest move, Ford tricked the stockholders into selling him their shares for less than they were worth. In 1919, Ford started the rumor that he was leaving the company to start a competing business. Panicky stockholders searched for buyers for their stock.

### The Dodge Brothers

John and Horace Dodge had a long relationship with the Ford Motor Company. They were stockholders in the company from the beginning. In addition, the Dodge brothers owned a manufacturing business that supplied parts for many of Ford's cars. John Dodge was a member of Ford's board of directors. However, by the summer of 1913, the Dodge brothers had grown tired of Henry Ford's tight control of the company. John quit his position on the board, and the brothers closed all their company's accounts with Ford.

The Dodge brothers kept their stock, however, which made up 10 percent of the company's total shares. In 1919, Ford bought out the Dodge brothers' shares. For their initial investment of $10,000, the brothers received $9.5 million in dividends between 1903 and 1919. When they sold their shares in 1919, they received an additional $25 million.

The Dodge brothers founded their own car company to compete with Ford. Their first cars rolled out in 1915. Surviving through multiple mergers and changes in ownership, the cars and trucks that bear their name today are part of the Chrysler car company.

Conveniently, a nameless buyer stepped forward. The stockholders dumped their shares at a low price. Later, they discovered that the buyer was Henry Ford, working through other company executives.

In sole control of the company, Ford flung himself into expansion. The result of all his hard work would be the largest industrial complex the world had ever seen: River Rouge in Dearborn, Michigan. Ford envisioned that this new plant would churn out 10,000 cars per day.

In working toward this goal, Ford used a system of vertical integration. A company that is horizontally integrated tries to control all the business in its industry. A company that is vertically integrated, however, seeks to control the production process, from providing the raw materials to selling the finished product. Vertical integration puts all the steps in the manufacturing process in one location. Ford saw that it was possible to save a lot of money by controlling every step in making a car, as well as its distribution and sale. The new plant at River Rouge would be specially designed to contain the entire process. Construction began during World War I. The plant gradually began producing parts as its buildings were completed throughout the 1920s. ⌐

A container of molten steel is emptied at Ford's River Rouge plant in 1924.

*Henry Ford in 1924, next to the first and the ten-millionth
Model T Ford automobiles*

# HARD TIMES

For Henry Ford, the 1920s were marked by
uncertainty, disagreement, and a loss of
the vision that had made him great in the previous
decade. Starting with James Couzens and the Dodge
brothers, a large group of experienced executives

and managers left or were fired from the Ford Motor Company during this time. Most left because they could no longer put up with Ford's difficult management style. Ford demanded total loyalty from his employees. In his mind, this meant they could not question his decisions.

Charles Sorensen and Harry Bennett, the new head of security at the Ford Motor Company, spread fear among the employees. This began when Sorensen became the head of the new plant at River Rouge. Both men were known for being intimidating, firing people for no reason, and blindly obeying Ford's orders.

Edsel Ford and his second-in-command, Ernest Kanzler, frequently butted heads with Sorensen and Bennett. One of Edsel's first acts after becoming president of the company in 1919 was to fire Sorensen. However, he quickly learned how little power he actually had when his father gave Sorensen his job back.

## New Competition

Henry Ford's refusal to listen to new ideas came at just the wrong time for the company. As one manager described the atmosphere at the company in the early 1920s, "It was a matter of doing what you were told."[1] The Ford Motor Company was still selling a huge number of cars each year. Yet, as the 1920s progressed, the company was selling a smaller percentage of the total number of cars sold.

Ford especially faced competition from General Motors. Former Ford executive William Knudsen had joined General Motors after being fired from Ford in 1921. Knudsen positioned his new company and its car line, Chevrolet, to directly challenge Ford.

General Motors had several advantages over Ford during the 1920s. First, it

### Ford Sues the *Chicago Tribune*

On June 25, 1916, an article in the *Chicago Tribune* attacked Henry Ford for being unpatriotic. The article stated that he gave away the jobs of some National Guard members who had been sent to Mexico. Ford had taken no such action and objected to the language used to describe him in the article. He sued the newspaper, and the trial began in May 1919.

The *Tribune* had called Ford an "ignorant idealist" and an anarchist, so its lawyers tried to prove that he actually was poorly informed and against government.[2] When the lawyers questioned Ford about U.S. history and culture, he answered almost every question incorrectly. One lawyer asked in frustration if Ford could even read. Ford replied, "I am not a fast reader . . . and I would make a botch of it."[3]

Ford was made fun of in newspapers across the United States. However, everyday people had real sympathy for him. They saw him as one of their own and believed he was attacked by smart-aleck lawyers over issues that were not important for everyday life.

The verdict of the trial was a compromise: The newspaper was found guilty, but it only had to pay Ford six cents in damages.

developed a system in which buyers could pay for
their new cars a little at a time on an installment
plan. Before this, a buyer had to have cash to buy
a car because banks did not give auto loans. Ford
buyers still had to pay cash.

Second, General Motors was the first car
company to give buyers credit for trading in their
old cars. Before the 1920s, roads were generally
so terrible that a car more than a few years old was
practically ruined from driving. Ten years later,
roads had improved, so used cars were in good
enough condition to be resold. The market for used
cars had the potential to ruin Ford. Because the
Model T stayed basically the same from year to year,
consumers had no reason to pay full price for a new
car when a used car was available for half the price.
By giving customers credit for their old cars—often,
Model Ts—General Motors encouraged previous
Ford customers to trade up.

Third, General Motors put out a new model
of automobile each year. Doing so made sure that
consumers would always have a reason to pay full
price for a new version.

Finally, General Motors marketed its Chevrolets
as new and desirable. The cars were shown as bright

red and sleek in advertisements, even though they were available in a rainbow of colors. Another selling point was that the Chevrolet was a fully enclosed car, unlike the Model T, which exposed its passengers to the weather. The new and exciting Chevrolet stood in direct contrast to the old-fashioned, unstylish Model T.

Edsel Ford and Ernest Kanzler understood the threat posed by General Motors and its Chevrolet. They knew the automobile business was changing and that their company would have to change with it. Henry Ford, however, refused to hear of giving up the Model T. In 1926, he made minor improvements and added two colors—green and red—but he stood firm on his decision.

## Outside Interests

In the meantime, the Ford Motor Company's troubles continued.

---

**Ford for President?**

Beginning in 1916, a group of people started calling for Henry Ford to run for president of the United States. Their cry of "Draft Henry" had little effect until 1922.[4] At that time, President Warren Harding was very unpopular. Many people thought that, if nothing else, Ford could not do a worse job than the current president.

Ford held back his anti-Semitic views during this time to avoid angering voters. His autobiography, *My Life and Work*, was published during 1922 and further spread his beliefs. However, Harding died in 1923, and his successor, Calvin Coolidge, was much more popular. Ford's chances of reaching the presidency faded away, and he stopped campaigning before the race really began.

*Henry Ford and Thomas Edison, 1929*

Although no one was allowed to make a decision without Henry Ford's approval, he was absent from the company for long stretches of time during the 1920s and 1930s. He had developed a number of other interests, and he devoted a lot of time to them instead of his car company. For instance, Ford developed tractors and airplanes as sideline

Evangeline

**Evangeline**

Henry Ford met Evange-line Côté when she joined the Ford Motor Company as an office assistant in 1909. She had a magnetic personality and was one of the few people who was not afraid to stand up to Ford when he was wrong. She became his mistress and remained so even as Ford set up her marriage to another employee, Ray Dah-linger, in 1917.

In 1923, Evangeline gave birth to a son, John Dahlinger. Ford treated John as his son, but Evan-geline never said if she knew which man was the boy's biological father. Evangeline and Henry's relationship continued with Clara Ford's silent acceptance until Ford's death.

products. He was also interested in using chemicals to improve farming, and he funded scientists who researched new uses for soybeans. He founded a trade school to prepare young adults for jobs in industry. His company hospital and store became models for modern hospitals and supermarkets. In addition, Henry and Clara Ford gave huge sums of money to a variety of charities and causes.

After World War I, Ford bought a newspaper, the *Dearborn Independent*, to publicize his views on a range of social and economic topics. Ford often used the paper to spread his paranoid views about Jews. He finally went too far by saying nasty things about a Jewish lawyer, Aaron Sapiro, and Sapiro sued him in 1925. After the case ended in a mistrial in 1927, Ford wrote a long apology to Sapiro in his newspaper, taking back everything he had said about

Jews. That was the end of the *Dearborn Independent,* which Ford closed on December 31, 1927. However, it was not the end of Ford's anti-Semitism. It is likely that he held anti-Semitic views for the rest of his life.

During this time, Ford became involved in a number of unusual causes and ideas. In addition to his interests in folk dancing, fad diets, and unusual spiritual beliefs, he became obsessed with re-creating the past. He spent large amounts of time and money seeking and buying antiques and collectibles. He spent the 1920s organizing his collection into a huge museum complex with replicas of famous buildings, called Greenfield Village. By the 1930s, Ford spent more time at the museum than at his factories.

## EDSEL PUSHES BACK

In 1926, Edsel Ford and Ernest Kanzler began to push harder for

### Ford and African Americans

Unusual for a white man of the time, Ford believed in equal wages and mostly equal opportunities for African Americans. In 1926, 10 percent of Ford's workers were African Americans. More black Americans worked for Ford than at all the other car companies combined. These workers labored alongside white workers for the same pay, and some even held positions of authority over white workers. Ford also gave large sums of money to African American schools and communities in Detroit and in the South.

Henry Ford to allow a new model of car to be made.
The company had purchased the failing Lincoln
Company and taken over production of its luxury
cars. And with each passing year, the Model T was
growing more and more outdated. Kanzler was soon
fired for speaking out, leaving Edsel to fight his
father alone.

Henry Ford refused to change until 1927, when
General Motors began taking large chunks of his
company's business. In the first few months of 1927,
the Ford Motor Company at last began to work on
a new model of car. By May, River Rouge was shut
down in order to rebuild the machines to produce
the new car.

People were excited across the United States.
Ford's new car, the Model A, was introduced with
fanfare in November 1927. Sportier than the
Model T and with many improved features,
the Model A was a success.

Even so, the years of making a single model
of car were over. The U.S. automobile industry
now followed the idea of planned obsolescence.
According to this idea, companies intentionally
produce goods that become outdated so consumers
will have to purchase new goods in the future.

Specific cars, all varying in price, were designed to attract people from various income groups. Henry Ford would have to keep making new cars with changing, distinctive features if he wanted his company to survive.

## CRASH AND DEPRESSION

Problems were beginning to appear in the U.S. economy. By the end of the 1920s, the country and the world were plunged into the Great Depression. This period of hard economic times started when the stock market crashed on October 29, 1929, and lasted into the early 1940s.

At the end of the 1920s, Ford's employees were not happy. Many were bored by the tedious work. Ford had stopped unions from organizing in his company, believing that they got in the way of production. Workers were also unhappy with managers such as Sorensen and Bennett, who used spies, fear, and even violence to get people to do what they wanted.

"Practically nothing of importance is secured by mere demand That is why strikes always fail—even though they may seem to succeed. A strike which brings higher wages or shorter hours and passes on the burden to the community is really unsuccessful. It only . . . decreases the number of jobs [the business] can support. This is not to say that no strike is justified— it may draw attention to an evil. . . . The pity is that men should be compelled to use the strike to get what is theirs by rights. No American ought to be compelled to strike for his rights."[5]

—Henry Ford

The harsh effects of the Depression also made life difficult for workers across the country.

Ford quickly raised the minimum wage to seven dollars a day, but by 1931, sales had dropped. The next year, Ford cut wages and jobs by almost half, even as he introduced a new car model. The car contained a V-8 engine, which was made of eight cylinders in a V shape. The Ford V-8 was a remarkable technical achievement, as it was a powerful engine that was usually reserved for only luxury cars. The masses now had access to a fast car.

The tension at Ford Motor Company boiled over in 1932. On March 6, a communist group held a rally and organized a "Ford Hunger March" to make its way to River Rouge. The marchers demanded jobs, raises, and social services. As they approached the plant, they met Bennett, who was backed by a Ford security team and members of the police. Bennett gave the order for fire hoses to be turned on the crowd. The marchers did not stop. Then, one of Bennett's men shot a gun into the crowd. The scene quickly changed from a march to a riot, leaving four people dead and nineteen seriously injured. With the riot, Ford's image as a friend to workers disappeared.

*Henry, right, and Edsel Ford with a V-8 engine*

*In the 1930s, Chrysler and other automobile companies introduced stylish cars that competed with the Ford Motor Company.*

# THE SLOW DESCENT

Throughout the 1930s, the Ford Motor Company was troubled by the same problems that it had faced during the 1920s. Company executives, including Henry and Edsel Ford, could not agree on anything, from small

details to large decisions. The elder Ford spent a
lot of his time away from the plant, but he would
not allow others to make decisions while he was
gone. Other companies were becoming serious
competition for Ford. By 1933, General Motors
and Chrysler had both passed Ford in annual sales.
At Ford, tension between management and workers
grew worse.

## WORKER WARS

With Henry Ford's approval,
Harry Bennett grabbed more power
in the company in the 1930s.
According to the *New York Times*, the
security staff led by Bennett was "the
largest private army in the world."[1]
With this army, Bennett intended to
keep unions from organizing in the
company. Another violent incident
was not far off, however.

On May 26, 1937, Walter Reuther
led a small group of organizers
toward River Rouge to pass out union
information to the workers at Ford
Motor Company. Clara and Edsel

### No New Deal

In 1933, Franklin Delano Roosevelt became president of the United States. Immediately, he began a series of programs designed to lift the country out of the Great Depression. These programs were known together as the New Deal. Ford spoke out against the programs, especially the ones intended to regulate business. He did not think the government should interfere in private business. It did not help that Ford had developed a personal dislike for Roosevelt. In the end, Ford's opposition to the New Deal did nothing to stop the programs but served only to hurt his public image.

both told Henry that he should allow the unions into the plant, but he would not change his mind. Bennett and his men met the organizers on the bridge to the plant, near the place where Bennett had met a crowd with fire hoses and bullets in 1932. This time, Bennett and his men surrounded the union volunteers and beat them brutally. The incident soon became known as the "Battle of the Overpass," and it caused a national outcry. Bennett kept the company out of legal trouble by claiming that his men were acting

## Harry Bennett

How did Harry Bennett come to work for Ford? As the story goes, in 1916, Bennett had just left the U.S. Navy and happened to accompany someone to an appointment with Ford. When it came up in conversation that Bennett had just won a street brawl, Ford hired him on the spot to head company security. This story is not likely true. As recorded in company documents, Bennett joined the Ford Motor Company as an artist and worked his way up to an executive position. Bennett was a street fighter and a gun lover, however.

It is easy to cast Bennett as the villain of Ford's story. Indeed, Bennett was a harsh and violent man who was cruel to his employees. However, Bennett cannot take all the blame for the company's negative culture, especially in the 1920s and 1930s. Bennett was the son to Henry Ford that Edsel was not. Edsel was a compromiser, while Bennett was obedient to Henry but tough to everybody else. It was at Henry's orders that Bennett challenged Edsel's authority and with Henry's agreement that Bennett fought the labor unions. Bennett seemed to believe that he followed Henry's wishes and acted on his behalf. As Bennett himself explained, "I am Mr. Ford's personal man."[2]

on their own because they did not want to unionize. Bennett's group beat up several other union leaders in the next several months.

But the unions and the workers persisted. The working conditions at Ford in the 1930s were not very good. Workers were fearful and insecure. They were fired for sitting down, taking an extra minute at lunch, or even "smiling" and "laughing with other fellows."[3] Bennett's security force also beat up workers. It is unknown how much the crackdowns and poor conditions were under Ford's control or how much Bennett did on his own.

In 1941, a huge strike and a union victory in the U.S. Supreme Court combined to finally force Ford to allow workers to unionize. Knowing he was defeated at last, Ford gave the unions everything they wanted and agreed to more generous labor terms than the competing automakers had provided.

## Another War

On September 1, 1939, German leader Adolf Hitler invaded Poland and started World War II. After the invasion, the United States stayed neutral. As he had during World War I, Ford insisted the United States should stay out of the conflict.

## Ford and Hitler

Ford was never a Nazi supporter or a friend to Hitler. However, Hitler approved of Ford's anti-Semitic writings. Hitler even sent Ford a medal in 1938, which Ford accepted. Ford belonged for a short time to a group called America First, which included some members who were German sympathizers. The Ford Motor Company had a plant in Germany, so matters were complicated. The company cooperated with the Nazi government until the Nazis took over the plant.

In 1940, a time when Ford was delusional following a stroke, he thought he could reason with Hitler to end the war. To prove that he was not a Nazi sympathizer, Ford helped Jews fleeing Europe by giving them farms on Ford land. However, many people considered his actions to be too little and too late.

Soon, despite Ford's stated views, political pressure convinced him to contribute to preparations for the war. Edsel Ford and Sorensen had come up with a plan to mass produce B-24 airplanes. One-time enemies, the two men had put aside their differences to stand up to Bennett. Finally, with Henry Ford's blessing, they built the largest factory involved in the war effort: Willow Run. The land was cleared for the factory in April 1941, and the buildings were completed by September. Production began in May 1943.

In the meantime, in December 1941, Germany's ally Japan bombed the U.S. naval base at Pearl Harbor, Hawaii, and the United States entered the war. Henry Ford threw himself into defense and the war effort. Patriotic but still with pacifist leanings, Ford maintained control in one respect: None of his factories produced deadly weapons. They built planes but not bombs.

*Edsel, Clara, and Henry Ford at an event honoring Henry's seventy-ninth birthday in 1942*

## MENTAL FAILINGS

In 1933, past his seventieth birthday, Ford was still active and engaged in his many interests, both inside and outside the company. However, he suffered from numerous strokes in the late 1930s and early 1940s. The damage from the strokes left Ford confused and forgetful. Yet even as his mind failed him, Ford still grasped for control of his company. Worse still was Henry's behavior toward Edsel, who was stressed and unhappy because of his father undermining his authority and Bennett

making his professional life difficult. As the elder
Ford became more forgetful, Bennett took near total
control of the company. Edsel repeatedly considered
quitting. He fell ill with terrible stomach ulcers and
was sick throughout 1942 and into 1943. He was
finally diagnosed with stomach cancer and died on
May 26, 1943.

Edsel's passing was devastating for Henry. After
Edsel's death, Henry realized how much he had
loved his son. Henry's mental state grew worse.
In June 1943, a delusional and paranoid Henry
Ford announced that he would once again be the
company's president. He made odd statements—for
instance, saying that the company would return to
making the Model T. Bennett continued to close his
iron fist on the company. Into this difficult situation
came 25-year-old Henry Ford II, Edsel's son, in
August 1943. Henry II started to quietly gather
supporters, preparing to take over when the time
was right.

Ford suffered another huge stroke in February
1945. His doctor explained that after the stroke,
Ford "had a memory of past events but not
recent things. . . . During rides with Henry
Ford [II], he would ask the same questions several

times . . . and of this Mr. Ford had no recollection."[4]

It was obvious that Ford could no longer care for himself, much less run the company. But he was stubborn, and he still relied on Bennett. The Ford family found a document naming Bennett as Ford's successor. It remains unclear, however, if Ford wrote the document or if Bennett forged it. Clara and Eleanor, Edsel's wife, demanded that Ford step down and name Henry II the new president. Ford gave in, and Henry II took full control of the company on September 21, 1945. Henry II's first act as president was to fire Bennett.

## A Man of Contrasts

Ford lived with Clara, remembering less and less, until April 7, 1947. On the last day of his life, Ford had a surprisingly good day. His memory seemed restored.

### Henry Ford II

Edsel's oldest son, Henry Ford II, was born in 1917. He was involved in the family business from a very young age. Son to millionaire parents, Henry II had everything he wanted growing up. He went to Yale University but finished without graduating because he cheated on one of his final papers. He went back to work in an easy job with the Ford company, and then he joined the U.S. Navy in the spring of 1941. He later said that he finally learned how to work by being in the service.

After Edsel's death, Henry II returned to the company and began to take his job seriously. Although he was only 28 when he took control of the company and had never managed a business before, he rose to the occasion. He remained the head of the company until 1980, guiding the company into its modern form.

He went on a car ride with his driver and ate a pleasant dinner with his wife. In the evening, however, his head began to ache. He lay down, and with Clara at his side, he died from bleeding in his brain.

Thousands attended Ford's funeral on April 10. U.S. flags were lowered in Detroit, and Detroit City Hall was decorated in black with a portrait of the automaker displayed. At the start of the funeral, all U.S. automobile companies shut down their factories for a few minutes.

Ford's life was marked by tension and contrast. He was a lover of nature, yet he believed in the progress of industrialization. He was a good companion but ruthless when people disagreed with him. He was a brilliant innovator, yet he held hateful prejudices and followed odd obsessions. He identified with the common man but fought against labor unions. At times beloved, ridiculed, and hated, Ford remains one of the most important people to shape the course of the twentieth century.

"His career was one of the most astonishing in industrial history. Nearing the age of 40 he was looked upon as a failure by his acquaintances—as a day-dreaming mechanic who preferred to tinker with odd machines than to work steadily at a responsible job. Yet within a dozen years he was internationally famous, and his Model T automobile was effecting changes in the American way of life of profound importance."[5]

—*Obituary of Henry Ford,* New York Times, *April 8, 1947*

THE
THOMAS MACFARLANE BIGGAR
MEMORIAL TO

HENRY FORD
1863-1947

PURCHASED BY THOMAS BIGGAR IN 1945 FROM HENRY AND CLARA FORD
THIS HOME PRESERVED AND DEDICATED TO A GREAT INDUSTRIALIST
AND GREATER HUMANITARIAN

1985

*A bust of Henry Ford located at the Henry Ford Winter Estate in Florida*

# TIMELINE

## 1863

Henry Ford is
born on July 30.

## 1888

Ford marries Clara
Bryant on April 11.

## 1893

Ford's son, Edsel, is
born on November 6.

## 1902

The Ford Motor
Company is formed
on August 16 and
incorporated the
following year.

## 1903

Ford's first car,
the Model A, goes
on sale in July.

## 1906

Ford's first big
success, the Model N,
is released.

## 1896

Ford test drives
his first car, the
Quadricycle,
on June 4.

## 1899

The Detroit
Automobile Company
is formed and Ford
quits his job at the
Edison Illuminating
Company.

## 1900–1901

The Henry Ford
Company is formed
but quickly fails.

## 1908

The Model T goes
on sale in October.

## 1913

A moving assembly
line is developed in
Ford's new Highland
Park plant.

## 1914

Ford announces
the five-dollar day
on January 5.

# TIMELINE

**1915**

The Peace Ship sets out for Europe on December 4; its mission to end the war is unsuccessful.

**1918**

Ford runs for U.S. Senate and loses.

**1918**

Ford steps down as company president, naming Edsel in his place, but still makes all the decisions.

**1932**

On March 6, a worker protest against Ford turns into a riot; four people are killed and nineteen are injured.

**1937**

On May 26, union organizers are beaten by Ford security.

**1941**

Ford is forced to allow workers to unionize.

| **1919** | **1925** | **1927** |
|---|---|---|
| Ford tricks investors into selling him their stock and takes full control of the company. | Ford is sued for publishing anti-Semitic remarks in his newspaper. | The Model A goes on sale in November, replacing the outdated Model T. |

| **1943** | **1945** | **1947** |
|---|---|---|
| Edsel Ford dies on May 26. | Ford suffers a severe stroke, and on September 21, his grandson, Henry Ford II, becomes company president. | Ford dies on April 7. |

# ESSENTIAL FACTS

### DATE OF BIRTH

July 30, 1863

### PLACE OF BIRTH

Dearborn, Michigan

### DATE OF DEATH

April 7, 1947

### PARENTS

William and Mary Ford

### EDUCATION

One-room schoolhouse near Dearborn, Michigan

### MARRIAGE

Clara Bryant, April 11, 1888

### CHILDREN

Edsel, born November 6, 1893

(possibly John Dahlinger, born in 1923, with mistress Evangeline Dahlinger)

## CAREER HIGHLIGHTS

Ford left home as a young man and learned to be a machinist through a series of apprenticeships. He designed his first working car, the Quadricycle, in 1896. After forming two failed companies, Ford succeeded with the Ford Motor Company. He became one of the richest people in the world.

## SOCIETAL CONTRIBUTION

Ford's Model T was the first car designed to be affordable to most people. It was the most popular car in the United States for nearly 20 years. Ford made several key innovations in modern factories, including the moving assembly line, higher wages for workers, and vertical integration (putting all the steps in the manufacturing process in one location).

## CONFLICTS

Ford encouraged fighting and competition among his company managers, including his own son, Edsel. During the 1920s and 1930s, Ford allowed an atmosphere of fear to dominate the company. Ford's political views were often controversial. He was an outspoken pacifist and anti-Semite. During the 1930s, he fought union organizers in an attempt to prevent his workers from forming unions.

## QUOTE

"I will build a motor car for the great multitude. It will be large enough for the family but small enough for the individual to run and care for. It will be constructed of the best material, by the best men to be hired, after the simplest designs that modern engineering can devise. But it will be so low in price that no man making a good salary will be unable to own one."—*Henry Ford*

# ADDITIONAL RESOURCES

## SELECT BIBLIOGRAPHY

Brinkley, Douglas. *Wheels for the World: Henry Ford, His Company, and a Century of Progress*. New York, NY: Viking, 2003.

Ford, Henry. *My Life and Work*. New York, NY: Doubleday, Page & Company, 1922.

Lacey, Robert. *Ford: The Men and the Machine*. Boston, MA: Little, Brown and Company, 1986.

Tedlow, Richard S. *Giants of Enterprise: Seven Business Innovators and the Empires They Built*. New York, NY: HarperBusiness, 2001.

Watts, Steven. *The People's Tycoon: Henry Ford and the American Century*. New York, NY: Alfred A. Knopf, 2005.

## FURTHER READING

Mitchell, Don. *Driven: A Photobiography of Henry Ford*. Washington, DC: National Geographic, 2010.

Sutton, Richard. *Car*. New York, NY: DK Publishing, 2005.

Weitzman, David. *Model T: How Henry Ford Built a Legend*. New York, NY: Crown, 2002.

## WEB LINKS

To learn more about Henry Ford, visit ABDO Publishing Company online at **www.abdopublishing.com**. Web sites about Henry Ford are featured on our Book Links page. These links are routinely monitored and updated to provide the most current information available.

## Places To Visit

**Edsel and Eleanor Ford House**
1100 Lake Shore Road, Grosse Pointe Shores, MI 48236
313-884-4222
www.fordhouse.org/index.html
The Edsel and Eleanor Ford House includes fine art and antiques
and features tours, classes, and special events.

**Fair Lane, Henry Ford Estate**
4901 Evergreen Road, Dearborn, MI 48128
313-593-5590
www.henryfordestate.org
Henry Ford's huge estate includes his historic house and Clara's
extensive gardens.

**The Henry Ford**
20900 Oakwood Boulevard, Dearborn, MI 48124-5029
313-982-6001
www.thehenryford.org
The museum complex includes Ford's own Greenfield Village as
well as the Henry Ford Museum, the River Rouge factory, an IMAX
theater, and a research center.

# Glossary

**accelerator**
> The pedal that, when pushed down, makes a car move and go faster.

**alloy**
> A metal that is a mix of two or more metals.

**anarchist**
> A person who wants there to be no government.

**anti-Semitic**
> Prejudiced against people of Jewish faith or ancestry.

**assembly line**
> A manufacturing system in which the product moves from worker to worker, each of whom completes one step of the process.

**conveyor belt**
> A moving surface that takes a product from one worker to another in an assembly line.

**cylinder**
> In an automobile engine, the tube-shaped parts where the fuel burns.

**delusional**
> Having false or mistaken beliefs; considered a sign of a mental disorder.

**dividends**
> Money paid to a company's stockholders from its profits.

**engineer**
> Someone who designs and builds machines and structures.

**flywheel**
> In an automobile engine, a gear that helps the engine move the car.

**generator**
> A device that makes electricity.

**incorporate**
> To officially and legally begin a corporation.

**installment plan**
    A plan that lets a buyer take a product home and then pay for it a little bit at a time.

**machinist**
    A person who makes or works with machines.

**mass production**
    The system in which identical products are made in factories in large quantities.

**pacifist**
    A person who is against war.

**paranoid**
    Having extreme and unreasonable anxiety about what other people think and do.

**patent**
    A legal document that records who invented something and defines the inventor's rights to sell the invention.

**personnel**
    The people who work for a company; employees.

**stroke**
    A medical event in which oxygen cannot get to a person's brain, often causing permanent loss of memory, movement, or speech.

**sympathizer**
    Someone who shares or supports the ideas of a person or group.

**transmission**
    The gears in a car that transfer power from the engine to the wheels.

**vertical integration**
    The system in which a company performs all steps of its production, from the raw materials to the finished product.

# SOURCE NOTES

**Chapter 1. The Race**

1. Steven Watts. *The People's Tycoon: Henry Ford and the American Century*. New York, NY: Alfred A. Knopf, 2005. 69.
2. Henry Ford. *My Life and Work*. New York, NY: Doubleday, Page & Company, 1922. 73.

**Chapter 2. A Born Mechanic**

1. Steven Watts. *The People's Tycoon: Henry Ford and the American Century*. New York, NY: Alfred A. Knopf, 2005. 6.
2. Robert Lacey. *Ford: The Men and the Machine*. Boston, MA: Little, Brown and Company, 1986. 33–34.

**Chapter 3. Early Successes and Failures**

1. Douglas Brinkley. *Wheels for the World: Henry Ford, His Company, and a Century of Progress*. New York, NY: Viking, 2003. 26.
2. Steven Watts. *The People's Tycoon: Henry Ford and the American Century*. New York, NY: Alfred A. Knopf, 2005. 42.

**Chapter 4. The Model T**

1. Steven Watts. *The People's Tycoon: Henry Ford and the American Century*. New York, NY: Alfred A. Knopf, 2005. 134.
2. Robert Lacey. *Ford: The Men and the Machine*. Boston, MA: Little, Brown and Company, 1986. 104.
3. Ibid. 101.
4. Henry Ford. *My Life and Work*. New York, NY: Doubleday, Page & Company, 1922. 72.
5. E. B. White. "Farewell, My Lovely!" *New Yorker*. 16 May 1932. 1 Aug. 2009 <http://www.newyorker.com/archive/1936/05/16/1936_05_16_020_TNY_CARDS_000161110>.
6. Ibid.
7. "Original Ford Joke Book." *Vintage Antique Classics*. 1915. 1 Aug. 2009 <http://www.vintageantiqueclassics.com/e-books/ford-joke-book.html>. 5.
8. Ibid. 8.
9. Ibid. 30.
10. E. B. White. "Farewell, My Lovely!" *New Yorker*. 16 May 1932. 1 Aug. 2009 <http://www.newyorker.com/archive/1936/05/16/1936_05_16_020_TNY_CARDS_000161110>.

**Chapter 5. The Assembly Line**

1. Robert Lacey. *Ford: The Men and the Machine*. Boston, MA: Little, Brown and Company, 1986. 88.
2. Henry Ford. *My Life and Work*. New York, NY: Doubleday, Page & Company, 1922. 77.
3. Steven Watts. *The People's Tycoon: Henry Ford and the American Century*. New York, NY: Alfred A. Knopf, 2005. 140.
4. Henry Ford. *My Life and Work*. New York, NY: Doubleday, Page & Company, 1922. 83.
5. Steven Watts. *The People's Tycoon: Henry Ford and the American Century*. New York, NY: Alfred A. Knopf, 2005. 141.
6. Ibid. 143.
7. Ibid. 154.

**Chapter 6. The Five-Dollar Day**

1. Robert Lacey. *Ford: The Men and the Machine*. Boston, MA: Little, Brown and Company, 1986. 124–125.
2. Douglas Brinkley. *Wheels for the World: Henry Ford, His Company, and a Century of Progress*. New York, NY: Viking, 2003. 159.
3. Steven Watts. *The People's Tycoon: Henry Ford and the American Century*. New York, NY: Alfred A. Knopf, 2005. 182.
4. Douglas Brinkley. *Wheels for the World: Henry Ford, His Company, and a Century of Progress*. New York, NY: Viking, 2003. 163.
5. Robert Lacey. *Ford: The Men and the Machine*. Boston, MA: Little, Brown and Company, 1986. 131.
6. Steven Watts. *The People's Tycoon: Henry Ford and the American Century*. New York, NY: Alfred A. Knopf, 2005. 199.
7. Henry Ford. *My Life and Work*. New York, NY: Doubleday, Page & Company, 1922. 127.
8. Douglas Brinkley. *Wheels for the World: Henry Ford, His Company, and a Century of Progress*. New York, NY: Viking, 2003. 172.

**Chapter 7. Ups and Downs**

1. Henry Ford. *My Life and Work*. New York, NY: Doubleday, Page & Company, 1922. 240.
2. Robert Lacey. *Ford: The Men and the Machine*. Boston, MA: Little, Brown and Company, 1986. 154.
3. Henry Ford. *My Life and Work*. New York, NY: Doubleday, Page & Company, 1922. 161.

## SOURCE NOTES CONTINUED

**Chapter 8. Hard Times**

1. Douglas Brinkley. *Wheels for the World: Henry Ford, His Company, and a Century of Progress*. New York, NY: Viking, 2003. 290.

2. Steven Watts. *The People's Tycoon: Henry Ford and the American Century*. New York, NY: Alfred A. Knopf, 2005. 266.

3. Robert Lacey. *Ford: The Men and the Machine*. Boston, MA: Little, Brown and Company, 1986. 212.

4. Ibid. 220.

5. Henry Ford. *My Life and Work*. New York, NY: Doubleday, Page & Company, 1922. 259.

**Chapter 9. The Slow Descent**

1. Douglas Brinkley. *Wheels for the World: Henry Ford, His Company, and a Century of Progress*. New York, NY: Viking, 2003. 427.

2. Steven Watts. *The People's Tycoon: Henry Ford and the American Century*. New York, NY: Alfred A. Knopf, 2005. 447.

3. Ibid. 457.

4. Ibid. 525.

5. "Henry Ford Is Dead at 83 in Dearborn." *New York Times*. 9 Apr. 1947. 5 Sept. 2009 <http://www.nytimes.com/learning/general/onthisday/bday/0730.html>.

# INDEX

assembly line, 44–52, 56–57, 59, 60
automobile models
  the 999, 8, 28
  Model A, 30–31, 82
  Model B, 31
  Model C, 31
  Model F, 31
  Model K, 31
  Model N, 31, 35–36
  Model R, 36
  Model S, 36
  Model T, 34–42, 44, 46, 51, 60, 77, 78, 82, 92, 94
  Quadricycle, 21–22, 24–25

B-24 airplanes, 90
"Battle of the Overpass," 87–89
Bennett, Harry, 75, 83, 84, 87–89, 90, 91–93
Benz, Carl, 11
Bishop, Stephen, 22

Chrysler, 71, 87
Civil War, 14
Côté, Evangeline, 80
Couzens, James, 30, 32, 47, 54, 55, 58, 65–66, 74

Dahlinger, John, 80
Dahlinger, Ray, 80
*Dearborn Independent*, 80–81
Detroit Automobile Company, 6–7, 27
Detroit Dry Dock Company, 18
Dodge, Horace, 70, 71, 74
Dodge, John, 70, 71, 74

Duryea, Charles, 11
Duryea, Frank, 11

Edison, Thomas Alva, 25–26
Edison Illuminating Company, 20, 25, 26, 27
engines
  electric, 8, 11, 25
  gas, 8, 11, 18, 21, 25
  steam, 8, 11, 17, 18, 25
  V-8, 84

Flower Brothers' Machine Shop, 17–18
Ford, Clara (wife), 11, 18–19, 21, 22, 67, 80, 87, 93–94
Ford, Edsel (son), 75, 78, 81–82, 86, 87, 88, 90
  becoming president of Ford Motor Company, 69
  birth, 21
  death, 91–92, 93
Ford, Henry
  and African Americans, 81
  anti-Semitism, 66, 78, 80–81, 90
  childhood, 14–18
  death, 93–94
  lawsuits, 70, 76, 80
  marriage, 19
  political career, 68–69, 78
  political views, 30, 65–66, 89
  siblings, 15–16, 18
  strokes, 90, 91, 92
Ford, Henry, II (grandson), 92, 93

## INDEX CONTINUED

Ford, Mary (mother), 14, 15–17
Ford, William (father), 14–15
    16, 17, 19
Ford dealers, 47
"Ford Hunger March," 84
Ford Motor Company, 37, 69,
    71, 75, 76, 80, 82, 88, 90
    business trouble, 78–79,
        86. *See also* Chrysler,
        General Motors
    creation, 29–31,
    employee dissatisfaction,
        51–52, 66, 84, 87. *See also*
        riots
    expansion, 46. *See also*
        Highland Park, River
        Rouge
    five-dollar day, 52, 54–62
    sociological department,
        60–62
    strengths, 47
*Ford Times*, 47

General Motors, 10, 76, 82, 87
    Chevrolet, 76, 77–78
    installment plans, 77
    trade-ins, 77
Great Depression, 83–84, 87
Greenfield Village, 81

Hawkins, Norval, 47
Henry Ford Company, 27
Highland Park, 46–47, 48, 49,
    50, 57
Hitler, Adolf, 89, 90
horizontal integration, 72
Huff, "Spider," 10, 31

Kanzler, Ernest, 75, 78, 81–82
Knudsen, William, 76

labor unions, 55, 57, 58, 62,
    83, 87–89, 94
*Lusitania*, 65

Malcomson, Alexander, 29–32
Maybury, William, 27, 28
McGuffey's *Eclectic Readers*, 15
Murphy, William, 27–28

Newberry, Truman, 68–69

Oldfield, Barney, 28
Otto engine, 18

Panama-Pacific International
    Exposition, 50
Peace Ship, 66–68
planned obsolescence, 82

Reuther, Walter, 87
riots, 57, 84
River Rouge, 72, 75, 82, 84, 87
Roosevelt, Franklin, 87

Sapiro, Aaron, 80
Sorensen, Charles, 37, 49, 75,
    83, 90
Supreme Court, 89

transcontinental race, 41

vanadium steel, 36–37, 39
vertical integration, 72

Watts, Steven, 34, 50
White, E. B., 39, 41
Willow Run, 90
Wills, Harold, 36, 37
Wilson, Woodrow, 68
Winton, Alexander, 9–10, 29
World War I, 64–66, 68, 69,
    72, 80, 89
World War II, 89–90

## ABOUT THE AUTHOR

M. J. York has undergraduate degrees in English and history and a master's degree in library science. M. J. lives in Minnesota and works as a children's book editor. Her first car was a Ford.

## PHOTO CREDITS